Love Letters from Teens to Parents

Love Letters
from Teens to Parents

MARLENE RIDDLE

WESTBOW·
PRESS
A DIVISION OF THOMAS NELSON
& ZONDERVAN

WestBow Press books may be ordered through booksellers or by contacting:

WestBow Press
A Division of Thomas Nelson & Zondervan
1663 Liberty Drive
Bloomington, IN 47403
www.westbowpress.com
1 (866) 928-1240

ISBN: 978-1-4908-8264-2 (sc)

Library of Congress Control Number: 2015908674

Print information available on the last page.

WestBow Press rev. date: 06/09/2015

Contents

Dedication

To my grandson Calan Cameron (front cover), with much love and great expectations!

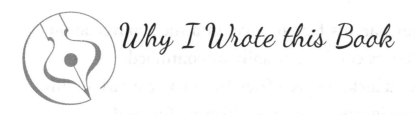# Why I Wrote this Book

Dear Teen Friends,

I know there are dozens of important things you would like to tell or discuss with your parents, but that you don't know where to start. You fear that they will react too strongly, yell, ground you forever, or make a scene. Well, there is a solution for that: write a letter, deliver it to them, and disappear☺! Give your parents a chance to digest the problem, meditate, reconsider, put themselves in your place, and remember their own adolescence. When they get back to you, either in writing or face to face, the problem will be half-way solved, and they will be more willing to forgive and assist you. Trust me!

Remember that your parents are the people who love you the most in this world, who would give anything to see you succeed and be happy. Isn't this a great invitation to start communicating? If you are shy and reserved, writing is the best way to start. Maybe, in the future, you will be so relaxed and at ease to talk to your parents face to face, in a nice conversation, that letters can be gradually discontinued.

Good luck, my teen friends, as you embark in this exciting journey! I will be cheering for you!

Marlene Riddle

If you like to write, and if you feel inclined to contact me, sharing your experiences and giving me suggestions on how I can improve my writings, you may reach me at:

MARLENE RIDDLE
riddlema@verizon.net

# Be Patient with Me

Dear mom, dad,

For days I have been thinking how to approach you and let you know what goes on in my heart. There are days when I wake up in the morning full of energy, determined to open the ties of communication between us. I am so sure that nobody else I know can replace you, when it comes to confidence and understanding. If I reveal my problems to my best friends, I am not completely sure that they will keep them confidential. Likewise, I cannot be certain that their advice will be completely for my benefit. Even if friends have the best of intentions, they may not have enough experience and maturity to give me the best advice. So, I have decided that, even if you do not approve all the things that I tell you, you are still my best friend! I don't mind taking the risk of disappointing you, even upsetting you, knowing that you have a great heart and will forgive me, giving me a second chance.

Please, be patient with me. All teens go through this stage of uncertainty, insecurity, and indecision. Just remember that I am growing up and, thanks to you, growing in the right direction!

Negative Pressure

Dear mom, dad,

When I am in a group where I am being pressured, I ask myself, "Is this really what I want to do, or am I doing it just to fit in? Do I feel genuinely happy, complete? Or do I feel like gradually distancing myself from the group and regaining my own self, my independence, my freedom?"

I know that, if I have the courage and determination to stay away from negative pressure, I will live a free and amazing life. On the other side, if I decide to stay in a certain group, just to fit in and not be a loner, the regret will come later on and I will lose a lot of respect for myself. I can figure this out now: when teens are doing something wrong, they don't want to be alone, so they get into groups. Misery wants company! People find strength in numbers!

Please, mom and dad, continue opening my eyes to what are the true values in this life! You have always given me my space, and I am so grateful for that! At the same time, please continue calling me to reality. I have great dreams and I want to pursue them, but I want to be convinced that you will support me all the way. I need assurance and direction!

Gratefully,

_____

Your Caring Words

Dear mom, dad,

What would my life be without you? Sometimes I think that I can sail alone, that I am completely safe in deep waters, that I don't need your direction and guidance anymore. I couldn't be more wrong! Even when we are not together, your presence is totally with me, reminding me of the straight path, whispering in my ears the choices I should make, for my own good and happiness. I have no doubt that, in the years to come, as an adult, I will always remember your wise and caring words, inspiring me, in the future, to also be my children's best friend.

I know that, in this life, we will have problems and adversity. Nobody is spared! Storms and disasters will cross our path, without warning. How can we prepare ourselves? Mom, dad, be happy to know that I feel strong and prepared! You have taught me to believe and trust in God, and nobody will ever take away my firm conviction of being protected and loved.

Thank you for trusting and understanding me. I will make sure that you will never regret that. I know I will make mistakes and fail sometimes, but you have taught me to get up on my feet again and, as a result, become even stronger!

Love,

_____

Marlene Riddle

# My Turn to Repay the Gift

Dearest mom, dad,

I hear many parents say to their teenagers, "When are you going to grow up?", while others say, "You are not old enough to do this or that. Act your age." So, I end up asking myself, "Do parents want their teens to become of age as soon as possible, giving them more and more responsibilities, or they prefer to treat them as children, babying them, doing everything for them, preventing them from strengthening their wings and facing this world with confidence and determination?"

In view of this, I have decided to stay in the middle, using my own judgment, and letting my good-sense dictate what I can and should do. I am sure that, acting this way, I will be able to be in peace with my conscience and, at the same time, please you and make you proud of me.

It was not by pure coincidence that I came to this world having you as my parents. You have been carefully chosen by God to provide me with everything I need, physically and emotionally, to succeed and accomplish my mission in this earth. You have been succeeding in your role as parents. Now it is my turn to repay the gift. You say that you are not perfect parents, just as I know that I am not the perfect child; however, we are doing the best we can to win this challenge and become victorious.

Thank you for being there for me every step of the way - sometimes smooth, sometimes bumpy, but always fun and gratifying!

Much love,

_____

Firm Determination

Dear mom, dad,

I left home this morning with the firm determination to make the most of this day. I thought, "There isn't much time left in my teen years; so, let's not waste even one day! Also, no-one has the right to ruin this precious time which was given me! I want to show the world who I really am: stronger than anybody's evil tricks to make me surrender to their terrible plans!"

Dear mom and dad, the reason why I value so much the time I spend in your company is because you have always trusted me, giving me guidance and support. I wouldn't be inspired to start each day of my life with so much energy and enthusiasm had it not been for your understanding heart, combining high expectations with patience and forgiveness. You have taught me that, when I do something wrong, to ask God and you for forgiveness. When I try hard and sincerely not to repeat my mistakes, I am rewarded by regaining your trust and confidence in me.

I love you and thank you for all you do on my behalf!

———————————

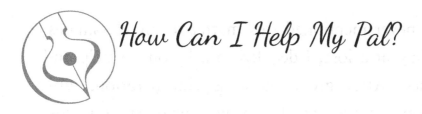# How Can I Help My Pal?

Dear dad,

A few weeks ago I told you that there was a guy in one of my classes who was very cool, fun, friendly, but that had a little problem: he didn't think that it was very important to take care of his appearance. I went to his house once and thought he had a fine family, but that they also didn't look like good hygiene was important to them.

The guys in our class liked this classmate, but some were a little rude, and hurt his feelings. That hurt me also. I really wanted to help him, but had no idea where to start. I thought how important it would be for him to create good habits, such as showering every day, wearing clean clothes, brushing his teeth regularly, having a haircut when necessary, all before he started looking for an after-school job. His parents were struggling with supporting a large family, and this extra income would certainly benefit their finances.

I never mentioned this matter to my classmates. Feeling at a loss, I decided to ask you for help and advice. After giving it some consideration, with diplomacy and tact being your primary concerns, you told me not to worry about it, that you would discreetly contact the appropriate school personnel.

Dad, I don't know exactly what you did, but what it was, worked perfectly! If you could see my pal now, you wouldn't recognize him! Besides caring for his personal hygiene, he also wears clean clothes every day. I believe that, when the counselor found out about the family's limited resources, she provided him, through the school, some new clothes.

This seems something so unimportant to many people, who only know how to criticize, but you opened a brand new door to my friend's future, dad! I will never know how to thank you enough!

With great appreciation, your son,

_____

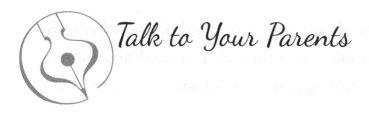# Talk to Your Parents

Dear mom, dad,

I was having lunch in the cafeteria with my friends today when one of them said he never opens up to his parents because he is afraid that they may get mad, punish him, or overreact. Some of the teens in the group agreed that it is very hard for them to talk to their parents.

A recent survey revealed that 51% of teens are afraid of talking to their parents, and that 54% are afraid of talking to their teachers about personal problems. I told my friends how lucky I am that you, mom and dad, always encouraged me to talk to you, if I had any problems at all, and that you would not yell or make a scene.

Some of the guys in my group of friends were very surprised, agreeing that they would be very happy if their parents acted the same way with them, sitting down together and talking about their problems in a mature way.

I want to thank you, mom and dad, for being so patient and understanding with me and my siblings, creating an atmosphere of peace and harmony in our family.

———————————

Marlene Riddle

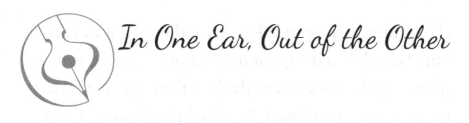# In One Ear, Out of the Other

Dear mom, dad,

My friend Jared was very upset today because his dad told him last night that he would never be good at sports. He loves basketball, but his team has lost the last three games by many points. Before basketball, he tried football and baseball, but was not very successful either. I feel very sorry for him, because he tries so hard!

I have read many biographies of famous people whose parents, teachers, counselors, coaches, and others told them they would never amount to anything, and later on in life they became famous inventors, writers, pianists, politicians, and world leaders.

I had a teacher in elementary school who told the students, many times, not to believe when somebody, even their parents, told them they would never succeed in life. She told us that, if this happened, to let these words "go in one ear, and out of the other." One day, when a new boy, with very low self-esteem, told the class, almost in tears, that his father always called him "dumb" and "ignorant," another boy got up, picked up the eraser from the board, and handed it to the poor boy. Confused, he asked the classmate why he was giving him that. The boy replied, "When you hear something bad about you, 'erase' it immediately from your mind!

I never forgot the lesson, and I am going to share this experience with my classmate. I am fortunate that you have always praised me for my successes, and shown me that each person has his own talents, strengths, and opportunities to become outstanding in his strongest areas!

———————————————

Marlene Riddle

Letters Unread

Dear mom, dad,

As you know, a student in my class lost his life because of a car accident not very long ago. His father was a pastor who had always struggled for his only son to live a good life.

After his son's death, the father found, in his son's drawer, a stack of letters he had written him, but that he had never had the courage to deliver them. The letters were mostly about his problems and difficulties in life. He had never had the courage to trouble and disappoint his wonderful dad. You just imagine how the pastor felt!

Mom and dad, I don't ever want to hide my problems and struggles from you! You have always been there for me, during my times of weakness and bad judgment. Please, continue being patient with me. I am trying, believe me! Let's have good conversations, give me good advice, always in an atmosphere of peace and understanding!

Thank you, mom and dad!

Marlene Riddle

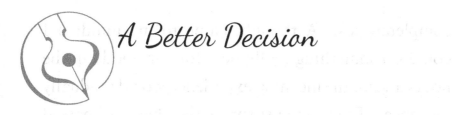# A Better Decision

Dear mom, dad,

Early this morning, when I woke up, I made the firm resolution to let this day of my life be worthwhile, despite all the temptations trying to call my attention. I wanted to live the best way I could so that, at the end of the day, when I was ready to retire, I would have a peaceful conscience and a feeling of joy in my heart.

Things, however, did not turn out just the way I planned. When I was riding my bike to school, this big student, who was also riding his bike, cut in front of me, laughing. I lost my balance and fell off, dropping my backpack and scuffing my knee. The big guy looked back and laughed some more. I wasn't sure if I should go back home and change pants, or be on time for my first class. I decided for the latter, but that cost me some laughs and sarcastic comments from some of the students.

The afternoon started smoothly. I tried to calm down and stick to my plan. The day was not completely lost. A thought came to my mind: if I could do something really neat for somebody in the hours ahead, the morning experience would gradually disappear. To my great surprise, the "big guy" passed by my desk in math class. Unexpectedly, another student, also a bully, tripped him. He didn't fall, but dropped a few books and notebooks. I hesitated for a minute, as the class was about to start, but then I decided to help the guy pick up his materials. When I bent over and started helping him, he looked up and recognized me. Embarrassed, he whispered, "Thanks, man."

"Alright! I thought. My day was complete.

I couldn't wait to get home and tell you what had happened. I had left behind my feelings of pride and revenge in order to have peace of mind. This showed me that I could overcome difficult situations and have control of my life.

Love,

_____

Marlene Riddle

Finding Answers to My Problems

Dear mom, dad,

I want to thank you today, from the bottom of my heart, for always helping me find answers to my problems without getting yelled at, or grounded for days on end. You told me that, when you were a teen, having problems and difficult experiences, your parents made great effort to be by your side, doing everything they could to help you overcome your most troublesome problems and concerns.

Thanks for always believing in me, and most of all, for letting me know ahead of time what the consequences would be for my bad judgment, so I wouldn't be tempted to do the same mistakes again.

Much love,

_____

 *I Will Keep My Word*

Dear mom, dad,

I want to apologize for not being cooperative in sticking to our agreement. You made it clear that I could go out with my friends as long as I came back at the time you specified, which was very reasonable. I failed to keep my word, and now I have to accept the consequences. I have done this a few times before, but now I know you mean business. I won't have the keys to the car for a while, but I also know this will never happen again.

Thanks for teaching me to have responsibility and character!

Affectionately,

_____

 *Great Relationship*

Dear mom, dad,

Do not underestimate me because I am a teen. Take me as I am now, remembering that I am still growing and learning.

I love you and I am very grateful for all you do for me. There is nothing I want more than to have a great relationship with you. I want you to be in every single aspect of my life because I know you want the best for me. When we are in good terms with each other, everything else in my life runs well, all my relationships are smooth, my problems are solved more easily. You are the source of everything good that happens in my life!

Gratefully,

_____

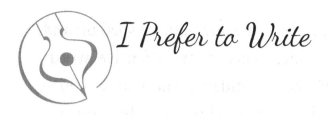 # I Prefer to Write

Dear mom, dad,

Some of my friends were brought up to talk to their parents about their problems from an early age. Since I was a child, you have encouraged me to talk to you also, but sometimes I prefer to write. I found out that writing you letters has really helped, because this gives you time to reflect and digest what I had to tell you without reacting in haste.

This morning, when I was driving to school, a young guy decided to tailgate me. He honked the horn, flashed his lights, and made inappropriate gestures. I tried to remember your advice, in case this happened to me. I didn't want to overreact, but stay calm, to prevent an accident. Should I pull over? Change lanes and let him figure out that I wanted to have peace? Stay on the same lane until he got tired and then decided to change lanes?

No cars were coming on the next lane, so I signaled and moved over. Fortunately, the troublemaker decided to stay on the same lane, but he sped up and, when passing by me, yelled some offensive words. It didn't bother me, confident that you would've approved of my decision, and knowing that your son was becoming responsible and mature.

Thank you, mom and dad, for your love and continuous support!

Respectfully,

_____

If Someone Ever Gives You a Hard Time

Dear mom, dad,

My friend asked me yesterday why some classmates, and even a teacher or two, decide to treat a student unkindly, even when they are treated politely and friendly.

I thought for a moment and then ventured an explanation: could it be because this student was particularly talented, attractive, smart, popular, very well liked, and some people were a little jealous? My friend, usually humble and simple, did not agree with my explanation. She said that she had asked her father the same question once, and that he had given the same explanation as mine. However, he advised my friend to continue treating everyone as nicely as always. This great Christian man also guaranteed that the situation would change considerably if my friend had in mind the following words, when encountering one of those enemies, "May the peace of God be with you."

My friend revealed to me that this worked like a miracle! Little by little, her "adversaries" became kinder and friendlier.

Mom, dad, I think I will try this, if someone ever gives me a hard time. It is a precious advice, mostly if we are living in this challenging world of teens!

Love,

———————————

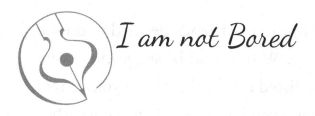 *I am not Bored*

Dear mom, dad,

Since we were little kids, we learned not to say "I am bored" around you, as this made you very unhappy. You would then remind us of a list of things we could do to keep ourselves busy, and at the same time interested and involved in some kind of activity.

When I was in elementary school, one of my teachers didn't allow us to say that we were bored as well. When some of us finished all of our work, we would read the words on a poster, titled: "Interesting things you may choose to do after your assignments are complete." This would give the slower students time to finish their work.

One day, a new student, who was not aware of our class rules, said that he was bored. The entire class looked at him and whispered, "Shhhhh…" The poor boy was at a complete loss as to what it was taking place… The teacher, then, kindly showed him the poster.

The mother of one of my friends decided to do the same thing at home. With the kids' suggestions, she made a poster and listed all the things the youngsters could do when they were bored or when the weather did not permit them to play outside. The list included board games, creative projects, competitions, some indoor sports, and so on. Occasionally, they would do something as a family, like swimming, roller or ice skating, watching a movie, or having a picnic. Sometimes, the family invited friends to join them. They lived a happy and exciting life!

Mom, dad, you also select carefully our recreational plans. You know that this keeps our family together, away from activities that would make us regret in the future!

Much love,

_____

A Little Reserved

Dear mom, dad,

I am writing to you because there are matters I find easier to explain on a letter than having a talk together. Maybe later on, when I become comfortable speaking with you eye to eye about important, serious matters, we will be able to have great conversations!

I am very interested in a girl in my class. We haven't talked yet, but she always looks at me and smiles. How should I approach her? How should I start a conversation? I am shy by nature, and this is a new situation for me. Tell me about your first crush!

My friend Rick, who is a little older and more experienced than I am, suggested that I start talking to her in a small group, for starters... This will give me the opportunity to get to know her a little better, and find out if she is interested in me. If this is the case, then I will be able to invite her out in the near future.

What do you think?

***

Please, Listen Carefully Before Reacting

Dear mom, dad,

When something is bothering me, I would like to talk to you about it, hoping that, before reacting, you would listen patiently to everything I have to say. Also, when I finish, it would be nice if you wouldn't get angry or yell, punish, or lecture me. Instead, we would remain calm, reason together, have a mature and positive conversation, so next time I had a problem I wouldn't have to go find another person in whom to confide, without being yelled at.

Sometimes we, teens, get in deep trouble, and when our parents find out, they say, "Why didn't you come to talk to me? Why didn't you trust me?" The reason is that we are afraid of getting into even deeper trouble.

Thanks for understanding me, mom and dad!

_____

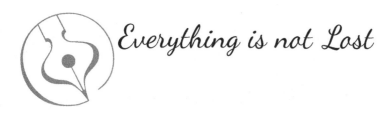 *Everything is not Lost*

Dear mom and dad,

I have been a teen for a few years now, and I have to confess that I am not very proud of the way I started. I have disappointed you many times, for no reason at all, even knowing how much you have tried to give me everything I needed. How could I have been so insensitive?

But - everything is not lost! Somebody said, "If you didn't have a good start, you can always have a good finish." Trust me, mom and dad, things are going to change! I have decided to make up for the lost time. Be prepared to have many reasons to be proud of me, in the months and years to come!

Sincerely,

_____

# False Accusations

Dear mom and dad,

I saw a movie where a teen was misjudged by his parents and the consequences were really awful! I know this would never happen in our family, because you always listen, listen, listen. I know of parents who accuse their teens of wrongdoing without ever giving them the opportunity to clarify the facts and present their own side of the story. There is nothing worse than being accused unfairly!

Even worse is when parents, embarrass their teens in front of their friends with false accusations. This causes a lot of pain and suffering! Parents should preserve their children's dignity and self-esteem, not judging them before they have proof. And even when they do have proof, they should not leave their teen completely crushed!

We, your children, are fortunate to have parents like you, who respect us the same way we respect you!

Gratefully,

_____

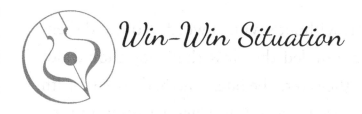 *Win-Win Situation*

Dear mom, dad,

I especially like one of my teachers. On the first week of school, she made a contract with us. She wrote, on the top of a poster paper, the words "Issues" on the left side, and the words "Consequences" on the right side. Then, working as a group with the class, she wrote, under the word "Issues," ten problems that could surface in the classroom throughout the year. Among them, for example, the students suggested: not bringing homework; using inappropriate language; fighting; arriving late to class; disturbing the instruction, and others.

On the right side, still working in collaboration with the students, the teacher wrote different consequences the students would suffer if they did not comply with the rules. Thus, when students broke a rule, they knew exactly what the consequence would be, without complaining or nagging. If a student forgot a particular penalty, the teacher simply pointed at it on the poster, without saying a word. Now and then, the teacher reminded the class that they should not complain, as they were the ones who had assisted with writing the consequences. Our class has been running smoothly, and the teacher never has to waste time interrupting instruction to embarrass or lecture to a student... Furthermore, the teacher remains consistent and predictable, never changing the consequences to adjust them to her mood at the time. It is a win-win situation!

Mom, dad, what if we do this at home?

Love, as always,

_____

# Enjoy your Ride!

Dear mom, dad,

I have been thinking a lot about this: I would like my teenage years to be the happiest ones in my life! Who said they have to be complicated, troublesome, difficult, tough, turbulent? I decided that nobody can make me unhappy, as I journey through such an awesome time of my life! It is all my responsibility!

This does not mean that there will be no problems, no difficult times. However, this too should be resolved with wisdom and good-sense. We need to delve into each day's challenges with courage and determination, finding joy in each success. There is power in joy! It is our task to seek contentment in this world!

It has been said, "Nobody can make you unhappy without your consent." So, I am going to enjoy this ride!

Affectionately,

_____

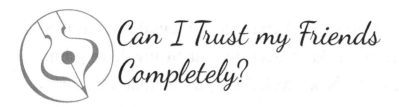# Can I Trust my Friends Completely?

Dear dad,

Something happened to me yesterday that really hurt my feelings. You know that Todd has been my best friend for almost a year now. We talk about our life, goals, dreams, plans, and aspirations.

I recently told Todd about a bad experience I had in middle school, and strongly asked him not to tell anybody. This morning, as I was leaving the cafeteria, I noticed that two guys were looking at me and whispering. One of them made a remark, which I overheard, and then they started laughing. I immediately concluded that my "secret" had been exposed!

I felt a deep puncture in my heart, not only for being betrayed, but for being let down by my best friend. I avoided Todd the rest of the day. I didn't feel like talking to him ever again!

Today, however, I changed my mind and decided to confront Todd, peacefully but firmly, letting him know exactly how I feel. If he tells me that he is sorry, and if I sense that he is being sincere, I might give him a second chance. I need to decide if his friendship is worth keeping.

Next time, I will be more cautious, before trusting my friends completely! What do you think, dad? Can you give me some advice?

_____

Keeping Family Matters Private

Dear mom, dad,

We have a small group of friends at school who, during lunch or recess, like to talk about their family, or ask questions about ours. I don't feel comfortable listening to them because, most of the time, their comments are somewhat negative. I understand that some of my friends are not very happy with their family situation and want to get this off their chest. I believe, however, that some matters are very private, and that those students should get advice from a counselor, a person they trust and who has some experience, or their minister.

I usually don't contribute to the conversation, but listen and show sympathy. If they ask something private about our family, I find a way of, very politely, give as little information as possible, and then change the subject. I owe you, my dear family, my loyalty and confidentiality, just as you do for me. I am so sure that you don't disclose to your friends what is so private and dear to me!

Thankfully,

_____

Marlene Riddle

Juvenile Correction Facility

Dear mom, dad,

Our teacher told us that she visits a juvenile correction institution once in a while, with a group of friends. This is a facility for youngsters who get in trouble with the law. My classmates were very interested in knowing more about the kind of life they live, and asked the teacher many questions.

At the facility she visits, the teens have committed offenses such as stealing, drinking, driving under the influence, taking drugs, fighting. The length of time they stay there depends on the seriousness of the violation. They all wear the same color of pants and top, usually a neutral color, and soft sandals. The boys have a short haircut, and the girls with long hair wear it in a ponytail. They attend classes every day at the facility, and the curriculum includes the same subjects as in regular schools, including P.E. They also have a pastor and a counselor.

I feel very sorry for these kids, being in a correctional facility when they are so young! Some will have a police record, and their future could be uncertain, if they do not change their ways.

Thanks, mom and dad, for teaching me how to make the right choices and have a good start in life!

———————————

Peace and Harmony in the Home

Dear mom and dad,

I like my brother a lot, but I wish we wouldn't argue and bicker all the time. You try so hard for us to have a home where there is peace and harmony, and we are not collaborating very much. We argued a lot when we were younger, but now we are teenagers and should know better. The wiser and more mature of us should be the one to say the last word and end the argument. However, we keep thinking that the one who stops first is the loser, the weaker one. How can we solve this situation?

Should my brother and I have a special meeting with you, to express exactly how we feel about this issue? Each one of us would contribute with ideas on how to solve this problem. I am sure we would be able to obtain great results and make our home a more peaceful and pleasant place to live!

Love,

_____

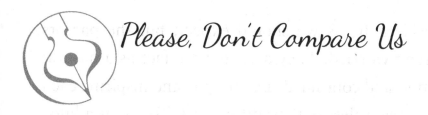# Please, Don't Compare Us

Dear mom and dad,

Thank you for not comparing me with my brothers and sisters, or even with my friends and other teens in the family! We are all distinct beings, and we need to be trusted and accepted just the way we are! Our personality and traits should be respected, as we have been molded to fulfill our special, unique role in this world!

We, teens, need lots of praise and encouragement for what we are, even when we are making small steps in the right direction. Some of my friends' moms and dads are constantly comparing their teens with other teens, or showing preference for one teen over the other. This hurts!

I read in a magazine about a lady who had quintuplets. When they were children, they all went to the same schools, had the same extra-curricular activities, traveled to the same places, were involved in sports. Their ability levels for different activities varied considerably, as we should expect, but the parents weren't worried. They accepted the fact as a natural matter, and continued encouraging and inspiring each child, regardless of their differences. Today, as adults, each one is successful in a different career and role in life, but all very happy and accomplished!

Much love,

_____

Marlene Riddle

 *To be Popular*

Dear mom and dad,

When I started high school, I could never imagine that I was going to encounter so many distinctive groups of students, according to their personality, tastes, and preferences. We have the rebels, the losers, the fun-seekers, the stoners, jocks, and those who just want to receive an education. These are from homes where they learn good principles. They are the best, the "elite," not always understood and accepted, but nevertheless happy and accomplished.

I cannot deny that I was many times attracted to one of these groups, just for the feeling of "fitting in." Some of those students insisted and pressured me into joining them, describing, in bright colors, everything I was missing. I had difficulty falling asleep at night, just thinking about how much more popular I would be...

Then, in the middle of the year, one of those groups got in serious trouble, suffered terrible consequences (including detention and expulsion), so I was ever so grateful for my small but well-grounded, sober, sensible group, who kept reminding each other: "Stay focused on doing what is right. Never get distracted!"

My group also has strong interests and enthusiasm for different things. We are deeply involved in many activities, but we don't let them interfere with our main goals.

High school has been a great "training camp" for me, after all!

_____

My Compassionate Friend

Dear mom and dad,

I was walking with a group of friends to a fast food restaurant, after basketball practice, when we passed by a bench where a homeless man was resting. His clothes were in a very bad condition, and his right foot was bandaged with dirty pieces of cloth.

One of my friends looked at him with sympathy, went in the restaurant, and ordered an extra-size meal, along with a regular size one. Then he went back outside and handed the larger meal to the poor man. But my friend didn't stop there. He sat down on the bench and, while eating, they started a conversation. The homeless man told my friend how he had lost his health, his job, and his family. Later on, my friend commented to me that those unfortunate homeless people need a friendly and kind word as much as they need food and clothes.

Mom and dad, I just wanted to share this with you because I really admired what my friend did. I think I still need a lot to learn about compassion and sympathy for the less fortunate in our society!

_____

Marlene Riddle

A Little Better than when you Found Them

Dear mom, dad,

Did you notice how customers left the "Top Burger" today, after you picked me up from school? I felt so embarrassed to see tables covered with leftover food, dirty napkins, spilled drink, chairs and floor in terrible condition! I wish people understood that fast-food places offer lower prices because they hire fewer employees, expecting that the customers cooperate by cleaning after themselves, leaving their area in an acceptable condition.

I am so grateful to you, mom and dad, for having taught me, since my young years, that we should always leave a public place just as clean, or even cleaner, than the way we found it. This is the same with bargain-priced stores. I feel discouraged to go shopping there, where there are so many articles on the floor, sometimes dirty and stepped on. Some parents allow their small kids to play with toys and everything else in the store, so they can have free time to do their own shopping without being disturbed… We cannot even walk through the aisles! This is a bad reflection on us!

Count on me to follow your example and never be a reason of embarrassment to you!

───────────────

Marlene Riddle

Keep your Friendships!

Dear mom and dad,

How many friends do you have now who have been your best friends since high school or college? One of my teachers said today that, when we grow older, if we have two or three best friends, we should consider ourselves extremely lucky! Do you agree with that?

At first, I believed that it should be more than two or three, but then I remembered that, when I reduced my group of close friends to two or three at school, my life became easier, less complicated.

Many students at school think that we should have a bunch of friends in order to become popular. What a mistake! It is not the number, but the quality that counts. If we don't choose well the kind of friends with whom we should hang out, pretty soon we will find ourselves acquiring their improper language, manners, beliefs, behavior, instead of the other way around. This doesn't seem like a good deal!

Affectionatelly,

_____

Marlene Riddle

Half-Eaten Cookies...

Dear mom,

About a year ago, when I was getting ready to leave for my first date, you gave me a hug, complimented me on the way I looked, and said, "This is one day of your life you will never forget!"

While we waited for my date to arrive, you told me about a lesson you had learned in Sunday School as a teenager. The teacher had offered the small group of girls some cookies, on a ray. One of the cookies was half-eaten, and nobody touched it. Later, the teacher explained that this is what happens in life: boys who want a good, long-term relationship never choose girls who have already been "tasted".

I never forgot that lesson, mom. You didn't have to say anything else.

With much affection,

_____

"Encourage Young Men to be Sober"

Dear dad,

I am having some difficult problems now and I would give anything if I could come to you and tell you what is wrong. The only thing is that I fear you will yell at me, overreact, cause a scene, humiliate me. That's the last thing I need at this point of my life!

The problem is that I started drinking, thinking that it would make me feel good and that it was the cool thing to do. Teens party and drink much more than parents know.

Well, I was mistaken. I don't feel so good anymore, and I think I am becoming addicted to it. I <u>really</u> need your help! I don't even feel confident enough to drive after a party, just thinking of the possible consequences. My friends always ask me for rides, and I think it is too much responsibility. How could I explain to you and to my friends' parents that I decided to drive drunk, causing an accident that could have killed their child? I cannot even sleep at night, imagining that you had found me in a hospital bed, hardly breathing. You don't deserve that! I want to finish high school without tragedies or adversities that could have been prevented!

Dad, I want you to be a part of my life. I am ready to receive admonition, reprimand, but also advice, calling me to reality. Please, be involved in my decisions, giving me guidance and sharing your thoughts with me. Many, many thanks!

———————————

Peace and Harmony at Mealtime

Dear mom, dad,

Something sad and disturbing happened last night, when Rob's mother invited me to dinner. We had been working on a project together for a couple of hours, as we had to finish it last night. Rob's father arrived in a bad mood, and when he saw his son's report card on the kitchen counter, his state of mind became even worse. One of Rob's grades had lowered slightly, while all the others had remained above average. But that was not good enough for the grumpy man. The entire dinner, he was yelling and humiliating my friend, to a point that Rob could not take it any longer. With teary eyes, he left the table, completely devastated!

At our home, mealtime has always been a very pleasant time. Everybody in the family is present for our main meals. Our conversation is interesting, constructive, positive! You, mom and dad, never call our attention during meals. If there is an issue or problem to be solved, a different time and place are selected. This probably contributed to our physical and emotional health.

How much I wish Rob's family could experience the joy we have eating and bonding together in every meal we share!

_____

 *Friends from Other Countries*

Dear mom and dad,

You know I like my group of friends and that we get along very well, but they don't like to hang out with students of other countries.

This hurts me a lot! I know teens of other nationalities who are fine young men, with good principles, great behavior, and excellent character! Why do my friends have to isolate themselves, as if they were superior to them? Our family has friends from other countries; we do things together, get along fine, and really enjoy their company! You have set a good example to us, kids, and we have a hard time understanding why we cannot be good friends. Some of our foreign friends are even more advanced than I am in some areas, and they are willing to share their knowledge.

I don't want to break up with my group of friends, so I am going to ask them if we can invite some of my foreign pals to join our group. If some of them say no,

I don't think I'll hang out with them as much. I'll be looking for friends who are kind and accepting of other cultures.

Marlene Riddle

# Embarrassed of my Family? Never!

Dear mom,

Thank you for bringing my math book to school, this morning. I left home in such a hurry that I forgot to place it in my backpack.

When you came, you stepped out of the car to hand me the book, and many of my friends were close by. I noticed that you wanted to give me a hug, but I walked away fast, a little embarrassed. Please, forgive me. That is what happens when we become teens. We avoid showing other teens the feelings we have for our parents and other family members, worried that they will make fun of us. We want to prove that we are grownups now, independent, mature individuals!

However, mom, when we are home or in a more private environment, please let's continue showing our affection for one another. I couldn't live without your hugs!

Middle Class Teens

Dear mom, dad,

We are a middle class family and don't have all the luxuries rich families do. You have full-time jobs and try hard to juggle all your responsibilities of a parent and an employee.

I have been thinking lately how selfish my siblings and I have been in expecting new clothes for different occasions without considering that you and dad also need to present yourselves well at work. Our budget is limited, and when you satisfy all our wishes to compete with our well-to-do friends, you always sacrifice and deprive yourselves of a much needed new outfit or pair of shoes. This is not fair!

I am going to find a part-time job and pitch in with some of our expenses. I am older now and able to work in a fast-food place, and still keep my good grades.

Forgive me for taking so long to mature and become aware of our real situation. Don't worry, mom and dad! Things are going to get better pretty soon!

With love,

_____

Marlene Riddle

# Out of Trouble...Almost!

Dear mom and dad,

I see and read so many bad things happening to teenagers everywhere that I wonder if there are any safe ways of being one without getting into all this trouble. I know that trials will come, but - can I avoid some of them?

This is what I have learned so far: first, I have to choose my friends well. They don't need to be the popular ones, the ones in the "in" group. I should decide to be friends with high- schoolers who have beliefs and principles similar to mine. It will take a little time for me to find the right ones, but it will be worth the wait! I might feel lonely for a while, but I should not be discouraged, but patient.

Once I find two or three good friends, we will be able to go together to sports events, dances, parties, movies... Likewise, I've learned that it is not a good idea to go to parties where there will be alcohol, cigarettes, drugs, immoral behavior. Not taking a chance eliminates a lot of sorrow and regret in the future!

The same guidelines we should follow when going out on a date. We should make sure our date has about the same principles and beliefs as ours.

Well, this is only the beginning, mom and dad. Please, add to this list and give me some feedback!

Gratefully,

_____

 *Freedom, But ... How Much?*

Dear mom, dad,

How much freedom should teens expect from their parents? When I watch the relationship between my friends and their parents, I notice that it varies a lot within each family. Some of my friends have considerably more freedom in their life than I do. Sometimes, I feel that this is unfair, and I want to complain, but when I think again I realize that each family assesses and evaluates the situation with their teens and then decides how much freedom they should allow. Also, this changes with time, increasing as their teens mature.

Mom, dad, you give my siblings and me the perfect balance of freedom and discipline, so we don't take advantage of the situation. My younger brothers and sisters want more independence, but they still don't have enough wisdom and maturity to make the best decisions. Sometimes it takes one bad experience for us to realize the reason why you, parents, are a little stricter than we wished you to be!

Love,

_____

Marlene Riddle

# How Much do you Love Me?

Dear mom, dad,

When you say to me "I love you," you say it like you really mean it! Thanks! You look at me, smile, your eyes shining, your tone of voice so convincing!

Teens not only need to hear that their parents love them, but be assured that this love is real! Actions speak louder than words. We can tell when "I love you" are empty words, like a disc, stripped of any emotion or meaning. When a situation comes when parents really need to prove their love, sometimes they fail, leaving the teen totally devastated!

I am grateful for having parents like you, in whom I can really count for giving me the assurance of your love, and supporting me any time I need!

_____

Never Discipline in Anger

Dear mom and dad,

I feel very sorry for some of the kids in my school. Some are rich, have everything they want, but their parents are very harsh when dealing with them. I believe parents should not be so disagreeable, stern, severe, strict, hard-hearted judges, angrily seeking out their children's faults in order to punish them. They should never discipline in anger, hatred, or indignation!

I believe that parents, yes, should discipline their teens, and these should never resent their parents' reprimands, reproach, lectures… Jesus said, "The Lord disciplines those He loves." When parents discipline their children, it should also be out of love!

Whether we fail or succeed in our effort to do well, parents should always tell us that we are winners in their heart, that we are gifts from heaven!

Mom, dad, thank you for not being harsh judges, and for giving me a hand when the path ahead sometimes becomes a little troubling!

_____

Parents' Divorce

Dear mom, dad,

I saw a movie where the parents of a brother and sister, both teens, were getting a divorce. The situation at the house was very sad, and the kids were quite depressed. They had always been a happy family, and the news of a divorce had been unexpected and shocking to the kids. They were confused about which side to take.

I know that this situation is very challenging to everyone in the family, but I think parents should try a little harder to make things easier on the kids. Of course, they should know about the problem, but the parents should talk to a counselor, a friend, or a church minister about the way they are feeling, and the details of the situation, and spare the children, who are already carrying such a heavy burden.

Divorce is not the only issue. Parents should go easy on the children about crucial adult problems and major crises in the family. Children already have problems of their own. I know we need to grow up and mature, but there are certain adult problems we need to learn how to cope with gradually, at the right time, so we won't be scarred for the rest of our life!

Affectionately,

_____

Thank You for Trusting Me

Dear mom, dad,

Do you know what makes me convinced that you are the best parents in the world? You have given me good guidance, since I was very young, teaching me right from wrong, and not nagging endlessly when I made mistakes. You respected and trusted me even when I failed you. The best feeling in the world is that of being trusted!

After teaching me something, you usually let me make my own mistakes, when they were not life threatening, so that I could learn from them. It's OK to make mistakes, and life always teaches us lessons from them. However, a bad choice can cause sad consequences. It takes years for us to gain trust and respect from our parents, and it takes only one instance to disappoint them.

Mom and dad, I will try hard to be responsible and careful with the confidence you have deposited in me! Also, when I make mistakes, I will accept responsibility for my actions, and not blame anyone else!

With gratitude,

_____

 *Happily Clean!*

Dear mom and dad,

There is a group of students in one of my classes who, every time they have a chance, like between classes or in the cafeteria, get together to tell bad jokes, or talk about very improper matters. I prefer to hang out with my own friends. Maybe this is because, at our home, I was brought up to watch decent programs, shows, movies, read appropriate literature, talk about acceptable topics.

When we are real Christians, we have nothing to do with immorality. We feel uncomfortable and out of place when it comes to unclean language or behavior.

Films and TV shows nowadays are corrupting, lustful, wicked material, being very hard for us to find constructive, inspirational content, or even a healthy, fun comedy!

Mom, dad, I believe we should have fun, mostly in our teenage years, and you have never deprived us of enjoyment, entertainment, an exciting life, all in a healthy environment. Every day, my amazement with your wisdom is renewed, and I will never be grateful enough for your firm and loving guidance!

Marlene Riddle

Remember, I Am Still Growing

Dear mom, dad,

I am trying very hard to adjust to and enjoy my teenage years, and I am doing it all for you! You are always investing so much in me, having such high expectations and dreams that I fear more than anything to disappoint you!

Sometimes I don't reveal to you everything that is going on in my mind and heart, trusting that I can solve my problems by myself. Right now, however, I feel a very heavy burden on my shoulders, and I doubt I can stand it much longer. I thought about confiding my problems to some of my best friends, but I am not sure they will understand or give me the right advice. I don't feel comfortable in revealing my most delicate issues just to anybody. I wish I could be like some of my friends, who find help successfully, but I am much more reserved than they are.

Mom, dad, I am absolutely sure that you love me more than anybody else in the world, so I want to tell you, in this letter, what I have in my heart. Please, be kind and understanding, as usual, forgive my bad decisions, and accept me as I am. Remember, I am still growing!

———————————————

Marlene Riddle

# A Healthy Body

Dear mom,

When I get home from school, I am very hungry! I go to the kitchen, looking for something good to eat, and I have to decide between healthy choices and not-so-healthy snacks. I usually feel tired to make myself a sandwich, so I decide for a bag of salty or super-sweet unhealthy foods. I admit that this is totally wrong! I am no longer a small child, and should be able to give you a break, preparing my own healthy snack!

Some school cafeterias offer teens two choices for lunch: homemade, healthy dishes, or pizza, hamburgers, hot dogs, fries. At my school, the line for healthy, homemade foods is always very small. Some students eat pizza every day of the week, and drink coke or other soda. Our teachers, mostly the ones with cafeteria duty, try to convince us to alternate our choices, but nobody listens.

Mom, I am fortunate that you, whenever possible, have a healthy, homemade dinner for our family!

 *Decisions, Decisions...*

Dear mom, dad,

We, teens, tend to rebel against your decisions sometimes, wishing to have full control of our own life. We fail to appreciate the blessing of having caring and experienced parents who love us above anything else, and are willing to make any sacrifices for our well-being.

I have watched on TV very sad stories of adolescents living in foster care or orphanages. However, many of them succeed, even becoming famous! Many find caring foster parents, who love them even more than if they were their real parents!

Mom, dad, I want to start appreciating your inspired decisions for my life even more, in the years to come!

_____

 *You are More Important*

Dear mom and dad,

Something happened during PE today that really impressed me! Some students were going to compete in a race, which was a very important event for this year. The favorite competitor for the race was a tall, thin guy, called Roy. He is in some of my classes and everybody likes him. He is just an average student, even though he tries very hard to keep up with the other students. His parents have financial problems. Running is Roy's only area where he can really succeed.

The second boy who could outperform Roy was Calan, also popular and well liked. The race started, and Roy and Calan were well ahead of the other competitors since the beginning of the race, maintaining that distance all the time. The crowd cheered with great enthusiasm! When they were very close to the finish line, Roy looked back for a second, tripped, and fell flat on the rough cement. He was in great pain. That was the chance for Calan to pass him and win the race!

The other runners were approaching them quickly. However, to everybody's surprise, Calan stopped, helped Roy up, and yelled, "Hurry, Roy! Hurry! Win the race!" With incredible difficulty and pain, leaping on one leg, Roy advanced a few steps and won the race!

Everybody cheered! The coach approached Roy, gave him a high-five and a hug. He also complimented Calan for his great sportsmanship!

Calan's kindness didn't stop there. He helped Roy to the nurse's office, called his own mother, and asked if she could give Roy a ride home.

I will never forget this day! Also, from now on, I will try to help those who need me, forgetting my own desire for attention, success, and selfish dreams!

_____

 *Diplomacy*

Dear mom, dad,

Since we were little kids, we have been taught not to fight, have harsh arguments and discussions, or even heated confrontations. How many times have we been punished, grounded, yelled at for our lack of self-control, be it at home, school, sport matches, or anywhere else!

However, when we look at the news on TV, all we see is wars all over the world! There are about 134 wars going on in the world today. Politicians claim that we should solve our differences using "diplomacy," and not bloody disputes among nations. What is diplomacy? It is trying to find peace, harmony, and agreement through mature conversations, and not physical force. This is true, not only between two nations, but also between two people as well.

I wonder if the great world leaders of today ever learned about diplomacy at home, in their young years! Did their parents explain to them that they could solve their problems reasonably, peacefully, using words instead of their fists? Animals fight because they have no alternative; they cannot use their reasoning or words.

I am already concerned with how I will be able to teach my own children to face their adversaries as wise human beings, using the superior resources that life will provide them!

———————————————

Happy Birthday, Dad!

Dear dad,

Have a well-celebrated B-Day, dad!

What a great feeling it is to know that, it doesn't matter what life brings, we will always be under your guidance and strong leadership! You are my role model and a great friend!

Thank you for all your hard work to support our family, giving us all the comfort we enjoy. Even working hard, you have always spent precious time with us, taking us on vacations, playing sports with us, taking us to church, and helping us with our school assignments. For all of this, dad, accept my love, my gratitude, my respect.

I cherish every ounce of attention you give me! I hope I will be able to succeed in my life, and fulfill all the dreams you have for me!

Affectionately,

_____

(LAST PAGE)

Printed in the United States
By Bookmasters